FIRE DOG
BAILEY'S
KID'S FIRE SAFETY BOOK

By Harry Martin
Illustrations by Jeff Vernon

This is a book about fire safety for boys and girls. These are lessons Bailey the Fire Dog taught to boys and girls (and grown-ups) when he worked with his partner, Harry Martin, and all his firefighter friends in Cal Fire and with many other fire departments.

Bailey was a big, very furry, Golden Retriever. While many fire dogs are white with black spots Bailey knew that, while he was different, he could be a fire dog. Bailey loved everyone, his firefighter buddies, big people he visited, but especially boys and girls.

Sometimes Bailey and his partner worked with boys and girls who had gotten in trouble playing with fire. This made Bailey very sad. He didn't like that the boys and girls were in trouble. He wanted them to learn to be fire safe.

Bailey and his firefighters also visited schools to teach fire safety lessons. Here are some of Bailey's most important lessons.

LESSON 1: FIRE IS A TOOL NOT A TOY!

Bailey loved to play! He played ball, tug-of-war, and especially in the water.

He played with his firefighters and boys and girls. But Bailey also loved to work. When he got his fire vest on he knew it was work time, not play time. Bailey knew balls were toys to play with. But the big firefighter's **AXE** was a **TOOL** and not to be played with.

Fire is a TOOL not a toy. What are some ways we work with fire? [cooking, warming our house, giving light].

Fire is **NOT a TOY!** What happens if we play with fire? We can burn ourselves, others, our pets. We can damage our home, our mom and dad's tools for work, our clothes and toys.

Bailey would want us to remember **FIRE IS A TOOL, NOT A TOY!**

PRACTICE TIME: SHOW OTHERS WHAT ARE TOOLS AND WHAT ARE TOYS.

Ask an adult to show you examples of fire as a tool.

LESSON 2: STOP-DROP AND ROLL
IF YOUR CLOTHES CATCH FIRE!

Sometimes accidents can happen if we are too close to flames or hot tools. If our clothes catch fire we must:

STOP! DROP! AND ROLL!

CALL FOR HELP, DO NOT RUN!

KEEP ROLLING UNTIL ALL FLAMES ARE GONE ON OUR CLOTHES.

CALL FOR AND GET HELP FROM AN ADULT.

Bailey would want us to remember if our clothes catch fire:

STOP! DROP AND AND ROLL!

PRACTICE TIME: WITH YOUR FAMILY
PRACTICE STOP! DROP! AND ROLL!

LESSON 3: IN AN EMERGENCY CALL: 9-1-1

Bailey wants his friends to help you if you are having an emergency. Firefighters, Police, Paramedics are our friends and want to help. If there is any emergency call 9-1-1. This will get help from firefighters, police or an ambulance. Practice making pretend 9-1-1 calls with an adult.

Tell the operator:

WHAT IS THE EMERGENCY

WHERE IS THE EMERGENCY

YOUR NAME AND IF ANYONE IS WITH YOU

Bailey would want us to remember:

In an emergency: CALL 9-1-1

PRACTICE TIME: WITH AN ADULT
MAKE PRACTICE 9-1-1 CALLS

(Adults, Show your child how to dial 9-1-1 on a landline and a cell phone. Pretend you are the 9-1-1 operator. Say: "9-1-1. What is your emergency? Where are you [children need to know their address]? Is anyone hurt? Is anyone with you? What is your name?)

LESSON 4: EDITH! EXIT DRILLS IN THE HOME!

In case our house catches on fire Bailey would want us to have:

EXIT

DRILLS

In

The

HOME

(E.D.I.T.H.)

If there is a fire or the smoke sector goes off we should **know at least two ways to get out** and stay out of the house. With your family make your **Fire Exit Plan**. Then have regular fire drills. Make sure everyone **GETS OUT and GATHERS** at a safe gathering place and **STAYS OUT**.

Bailey would want you to practice Exit Drills In The Home.

PRACTICE TIME: WITH YOUR FAMILY
MAKE YOUR FIRE EXIT PLANS

(Two ways out, a safe gathering place)
and Practice E.D.I.T.H, Exit Drills In The Home.

EDITH - Exit Drills In The Home

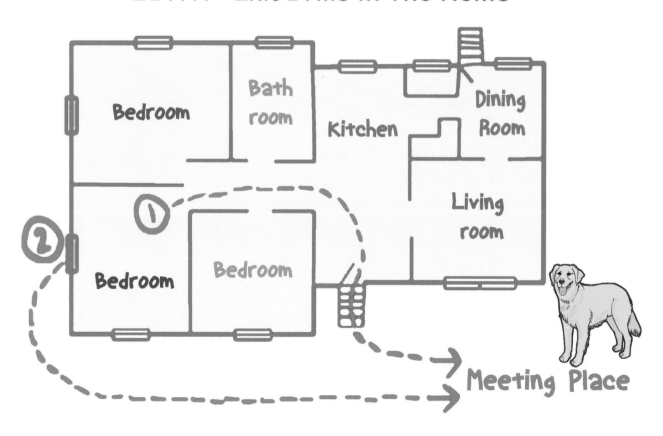

LESSON 5: CRAWL LOW IN THE SMOKE!

In case you are in a room or building where there is smoke—get out and stay out!

Get down low and crawl as low as you can (where the air is cooler and safer) under the smoke to a safe door or window.

If the door is closed, feel the door with the **back of your hand**.

If it is **HOT** DO NOT OPEN IT but go to a window and crawl out or call for help.

Bailey knew how to crawl low in the smoke and would want you to know too.

PRACTICE TIME: WITH YOUR FAMILY PRACTICE CRAWLING LOW IN THE SMOKE.

Take turns with two people holding pretend smoke (a blanket) and crawling under the smoke to a door. Feel if it is safe to open. Then remember your Exit Drills!

LESSON 6: CHECK YOUR SMOKE DETECTORS.

Homes should have smoke detectors on every floor. With your parents make sure your Smoke Detectors are working. Your house should also have Carbon Monoxide (CO, a deadly gas without any smell) Detectors. Have you parents check these too.

Bailey knew, Smoke Detectors save lives! He would want you to make sure your house has smoke and Carbon Monoxide Detectors that are working.

PRACTICE TIME: SMOKE DETECTORS

With your family, make sure the Smoke and Carbon Monoxide Detectors in your home are working, at least twice a year.

Bailey knew fire can be scary. But he was a very brave dog and he knew his firefighters were brave. He would want you to be brave and keep calm if there is any emergency. Remember your Fire Safety Lessons and be Fire Safe!

Bailey would also want you to make the Fire Safe Kid Promise. Many boys and girls promised Bailey they would be fire safe. Here it is:

"I promise I will not play with fire because fire is a tool, not a toy. And I promise I will help my family and others to learn and remember these Fire Safe Lessons."

Signed: _____ Date: _____

With deep and sincere appreciation for...

My wife, Randi Martin for her love and encouragement and being Bailey's mom. Jeff Vernon, Illustrator, for picturing, so beautifully, Bailey's lessons. Angela Hoy & BookLocker Books and Gwen Gades, Book Designer.

California Department of Forestry & Fire Protection, CDF, especially the Sonoma-Lake-Napa Unit. and Suzie Blankenship, Fire Preventions Specialist II, CDF.

All the brave firefighters, Paramedics and Police who were Bailey's partners and friends. All the boys and girls who promised Bailey they would be Fire Safe.

CPSIA information can be obtained at www.ICGtesting.com
Printed in the USA
LVIW01n2258160417
531050LV00002B/6